To **ALEX AND ERIN:**
Thank you for your contagious joy
and for reminding me to never stop asking
what numbers can do.
—Edmund

To **ALYSSA MONKEYFACE LITTLEBEAR TYRANNOSAURUS,**
the best One there ever will be.

Love you
More than the whole wide world,
More than the whole entire universe!

Your picture is on my fridge,
Your memory is in my heart.
—Houston

To **KRISTINA AND MIKO:**
In my book, you count the most.
—Brian

HELLO NUMBERS!

WHAT CAN YOU DO?

AN ADVENTURE BEYOND COUNTING

EDMUND HARRISS

AND

HOUSTON HUGHES

ILLUSTRATED BY BRIAN REA

THE EXPERIMENT

NEW YORK

In the emptiest space, on the blankest of page,

There exists so much nothing that it needs a name!

Like Zip, Zero, Zilch, or Diddly-Squat,

Null or Nil or Nada or Naught.

Can you think of nothing? Can you calm your brain

Till it's still like a canvas just waiting for paint?

Just the sound of your breath and the beat of your heart—

This is the *best* way for counting to start.

Now what if inside of that big, empty space,

Where once there was nothing, you dream up . . . a face?!

Or a point, or a dot, or a shimmering light

Like a lone shining beacon in darkest of night.

Now that the nothing is no longer none,
"None" needs a *new* name, and that name is . . .

ONE.

One is a person, a place, or a thing,

One head on your shoulders, One note that you sing.

If something's an "it," not a "we" or a "they,"

Then when you are counting it, **One's** what you say.

And that includes you—yes, you're a One too!

One person, unique in the things that you do,

In the thoughts that you think, in the dreams that you dream . . .

That's what makes you One—your identity!

Now back in your brain, in the place you see One,

What games can One play when One wants to have fun?

Atop the blank canvas, One *can* get around,

It can move to the left or the right, up and down . . .

But among so much nothing, poor One can't begin

To tell where One *is* from where One has just been.

One needs a friend to run *from* or run *to*—

One *needs* to compare! One needs *you* to find . . .

TWO!

And thanks to that thought, a new One has appeared!

But we *can't* call both "One"—that would sound really weird.

So say "Hello, new One! And how do you do?

I'll call you **Two,** if it's all right with you!"

Now, with your Two, you can tell which is where—
Maybe One's over here, and Two's *waaaaaay* over there.
Maybe One's going over, or under, or through,
Or like planets or atoms, One twirls around Two!

Two *loves* to be even—you know what that means?

It's like Two wants a twin who has all matching things.

A mirror reflection, the same on each side,

All evenly split by an equal divide.

When something's two sides are the same as can be,

Then *that* gets its own special name—symmetry!

Like the wings on a bird, or the ears on your head,

Or a sandwich that starts with two slices of bread.

But when you want something to go in between,
You'll need a new number, a number like . . .

THREE.

Say "Hello, new One! And how do you do?
I'll call you **Three,** if it's all right with you!"

With Three here to help us, it suddenly means
There's another place numbers can be—in between.

Put One in the front, Two between, Three behind,
And you've just invented a new thing—a line!

But if Two steps aside, so it's *not* in the line . . .
Oh look! It's a triangle shape with three sides!

Three helps make angles,
And "angle" just means
How wide your arms spread
When you point at two things!

With One and Two close,
While Three's *not* close at all,
The triangle's skinny,
Three's angle is small.

But if Three stays in place
While its friends spread out far,
The triangle's wide,
And Three's angle grows large!

Now picture that triangle, One, Two, and Three...
What if numbers trade places? Then what would you see?
It might look quite strange as they went on their way,
But once they're done switching, the shape is the same!

We've had fun with Three, but I bet we'd have more
If *you* could imagine the next number...

FOUR!

Say "Hello, new One! And how do you do?
I'll call you **Four,** if it's all right with you!"

Four makes a square, formed from four equal lines
Joined by four corner angles all equally wide!
And Four can make more shapes, like diamonds or kites,
Or rectangles—squares that got stretched on two sides!
Rhombuses, trapezoids, sharp boomerangs—
All four-sided shapes with all kinds of strange names!

Now imagine your square lying down on the ground,
With One, Two, and Three sort of standing around . . .

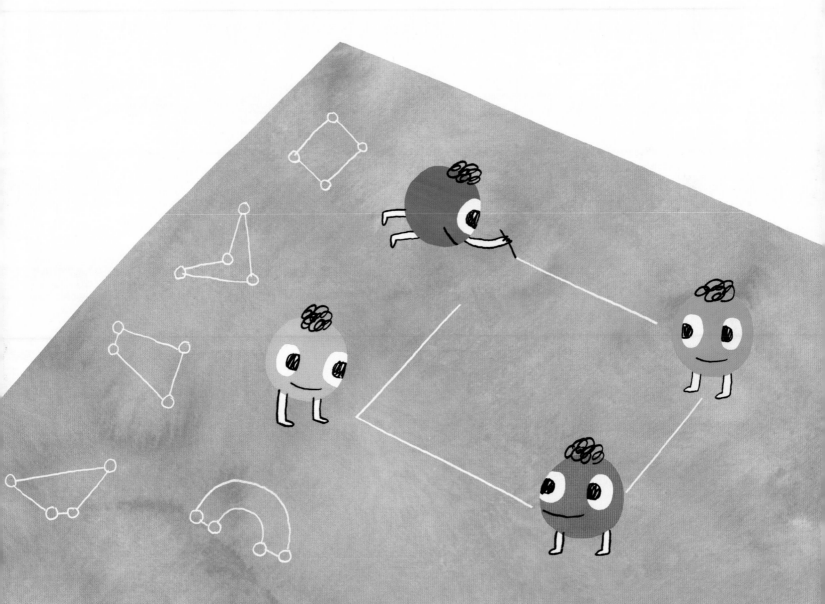

When Four, for some reason, flies up in the sky!
Creating a thing with three triangle sides,
And a triangle base—that's a bottom-side lid—
You've discovered a shape, and it's called pyramid!

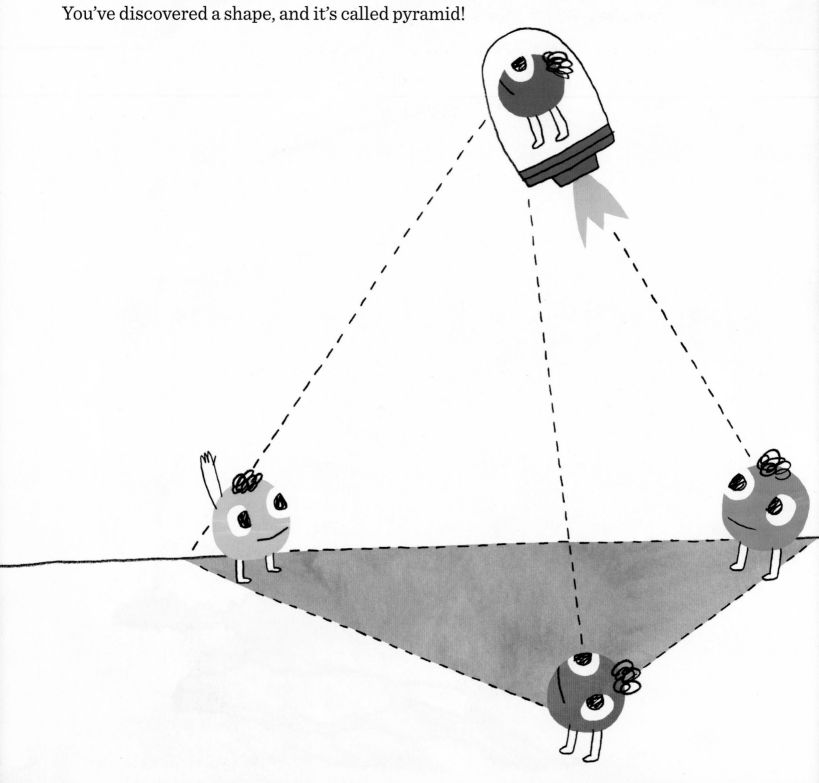

To make *un*equal piles, you can group One-Two-Three,

Then put Four on its own. But to make symmetry,

Take One-Two-Three-Four, and divide them in half . . .

It's a pair made of pairs—what a neat bit of math!

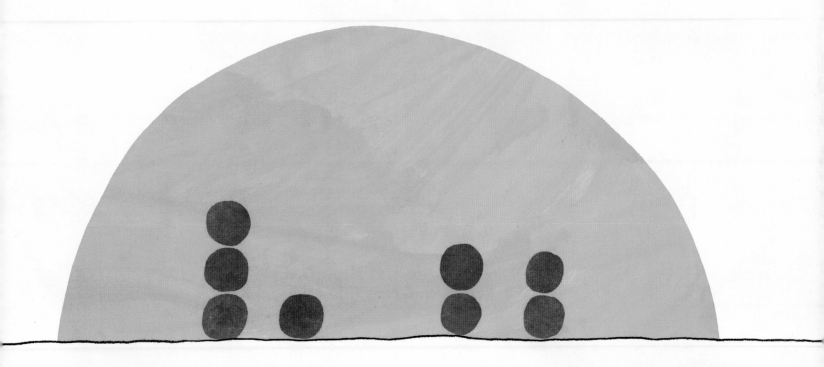

But that's all the splitting these four friends can do.

If you want to play *more* games, it's all up to you!

Imagine ANOTHER new number arrives.

Yell out its name if you know it. It's . . .

FIVE.

Say "Hello, new One! And how do you do?

I'll call you **Five,** if it's all right with you!"

With Five in your mind, do your Ones still connect?

Do they play in a pattern? A cross or an X?

Do the rest build a square, then make Five wait outside?

Or does Five join the end of a neat number line?

Do your numbers group up, or do they separate?
Just imagine the combos that Five can create!

If One pairs with Two, but then Three stays alone,
Maybe Four goes with Five! They're a pair of their own!

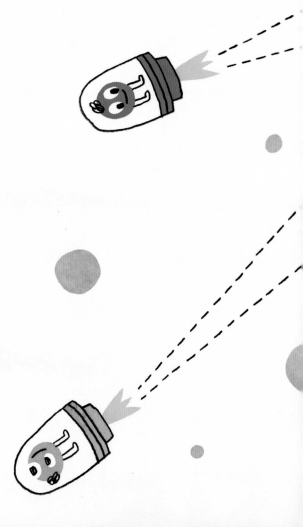

Set them all in a circle, with space in between,
Then out from each One, draw the shape of a V,
Connected across to the numbers most far.
Do it five times, and you've just made a star!

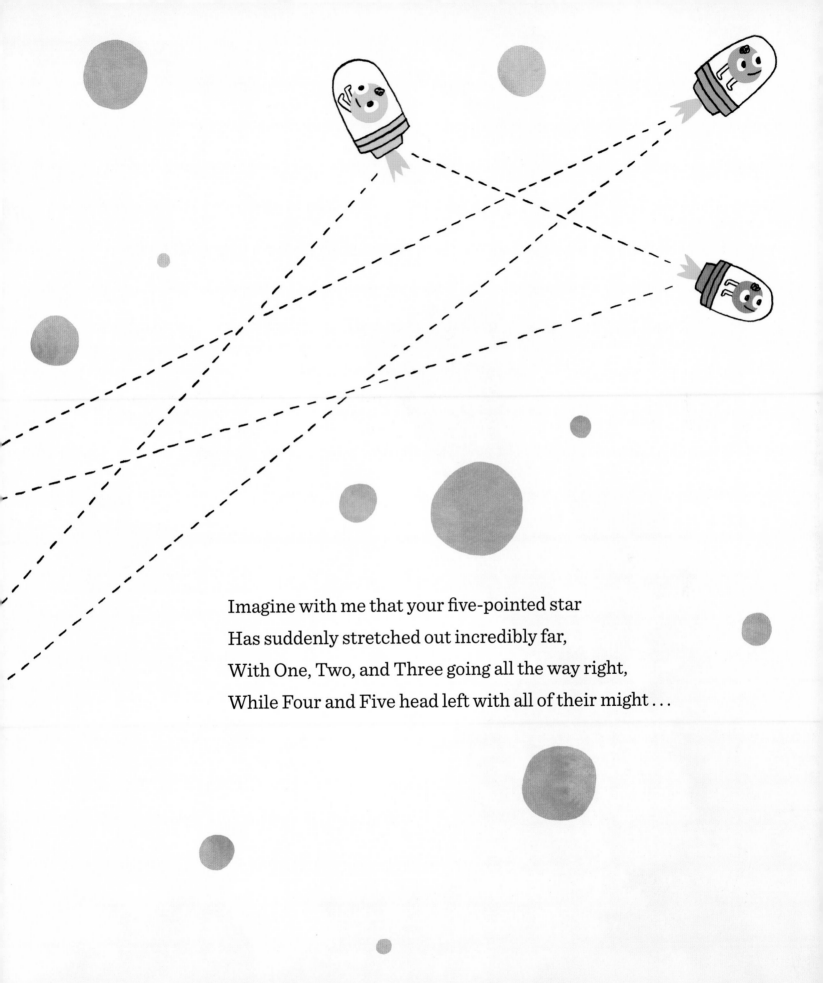

Imagine with me that your five-pointed star
Has suddenly stretched out incredibly far,
With One, Two, and Three going all the way right,
While Four and Five head left with all of their might . . .

Maybe, in *your* mind, they stretch far enough

That the star breaks apart, and your numbers split up!

One-Two-Three make a triangle; One-Two, a pair . . .

Our friend Five has vanished! But please don't be scared.

Zoom your view out, or your numbers back in,
And the moment your brain groups them up once again,
You've brought back Four and Five, like a numbers magician!
But that's no illusion—it's just called addition!

And if a new One joins the fun,
Don't you wonder—
Together, will they make
A whole different number?

OH NO!

We've run out of pages to play!

Perhaps we can keep going some other day?

But here's an idea—you can do it yourself!

When you've finished this book and it's up on the shelf . . .

You can keep counting! Yes, you can go higher!

Your lines can get longer! Your angles get wider!

And *new* Ones to play with means *new* shapes to make,

New patterns to find, and new groups to create . . .

Can you split them in two? Do they have symmetry?

Can you turn them to triangles, teamed up in threes?

Can you add your Ones up, and then fling them apart,

So the space in your brain's like a sky full of stars?

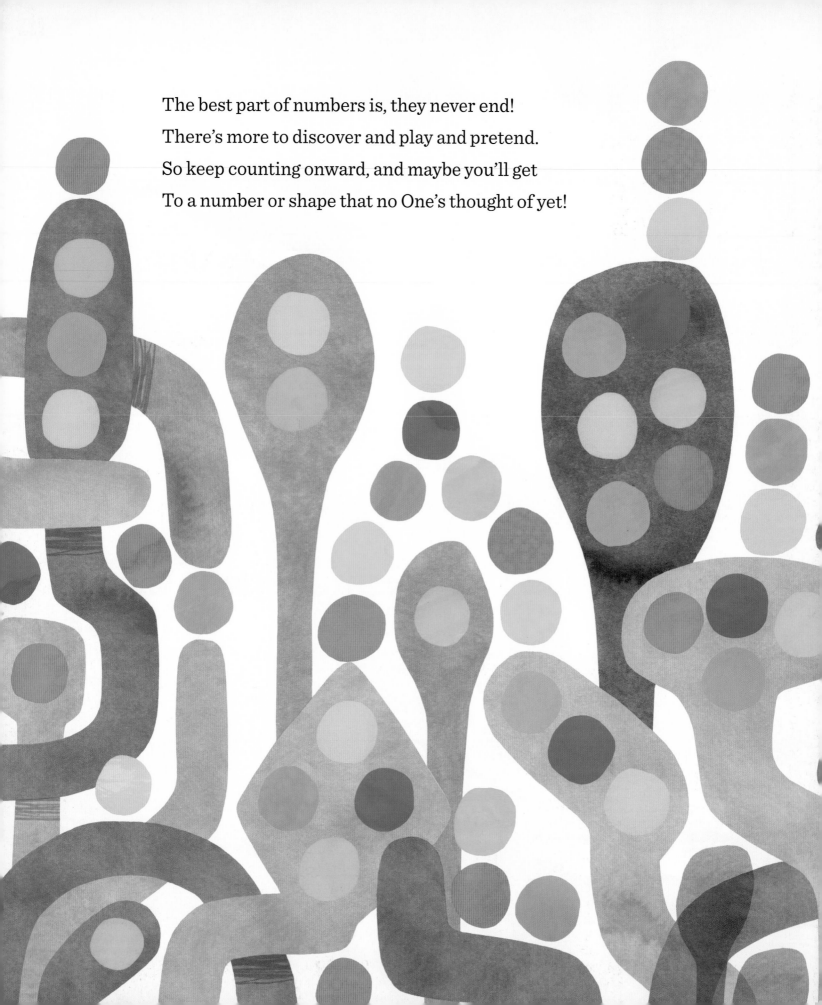

The best part of numbers is, they never end!
There's more to discover and play and pretend.
So keep counting onward, and maybe you'll get
To a number or shape that no One's thought of yet!

What number's the biggest you see in your mind?
Now could you add One to it, just one more time?
Here's the secret—you see it?—I'm sure that you do.
The One more you need is the *best* One . . .

IT'S YOU!

The Experiment, LLC | 220 East 23rd Street, Suite 600, New York, NY 10010-4658 | theexperimentpublishing.com

THE EXPERIMENT and its colophon are registered trademarks of The Experiment, LLC.

The Experiment's books are available at special discounts when purchased in bulk for premiums and sales promotions as well as for fund-raising or educational use. For details, contact us at info@theexperimentpublishing.com.

Library of Congress Cataloging-in-Publication Data

Names: Harriss, Edmund, author. | Hughes, Houston, author. | Rea, Brian, illustrator.
Title: Hello numbers! what can you do? : an adventure beyond counting / Edmund Harriss and Houston Hughes ; illustrated by Brian Rea.
Identifiers: LCCN 2020034100 (print) | LCCN 2020034101 (ebook) | ISBN 9781615196845 | ISBN 9781615196852 (ebook)
Subjects: LCSH: Counting--Juvenile literature. | Numbers--Juvenile literature.
Classification: LCC QA113 .H437 2020 (print) | LCC QA113 (ebook) | DDC 398.8/4--dc23
LC record available at https://lccn.loc.gov/2020034100
LC ebook record available at https://lccn.loc.gov/2020034101

ISBN 978-1-61519-684-5
Ebook ISBN 978-1-61519-685-2

Cover and text design by Beth Bugler

Manufactured in China

First printing October 2020
10 9 8 7 6 5 4 3 2 1